Unwrapping Content

The A–Z of Communicating Your Business

Emma Rundle

Copyright

Copyright©
Emma Rundle 2023.
All rights reserved.

No part of this book may be reproduced, stored in a retrieval system, or transmitted, in any form or by any means electronic, mechanical, photocopying, recording or otherwise, except as permitted by the UK Copyright, Designs and Patents Act 1988, without the prior permission of the copyright owner.

Contents

Intro: Content a bit out of shape? 5

The A-Z of communicating your business 7

There are several ways to read this book.

You can read it from front to back, A to Z, like a normal book.

You can flick through for inspiration, and find the page tips and quotes which summarise some of the content.

You can also take notes and jot down other ideas on the dedicated notes pages.

For T & V, who inspire me every day

Content a bit out of shape?

One of the main things that puts people off creating content (especially when they don't have bottomless budgets) is having the courage to simply get going.

No-one is alone in this. I have worked with many businesses who need the lifeline of brainstorming topics and thinking of novel ways to get their key messages across.

Not all of us work in visual businesses such as food or fashion. I work with lots of service providers who get stuck with the thought that their topic just isn't of interest to anyone else.

That's when some lateral thinking is needed. Consider your provenance, look at the stories behind the business and discover an unusual way to explain what you do using something that is more accessible to your audience.

Getting this right is worth the effort.

Today's shop window is the noisy, competitive feed of LinkedIn or your website or landing page.

Standing out is hard to do but good content will go a long way to reaching your target audience and growing your small business.

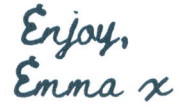

Enjoy,
Emma x

Always speak from the heart and be truthful.
Don't exaggerate or make claims you can't back up.

Engage with others, as well as creating content, so people can see the real you.

A is for Authenticity

I had to start with this really. It's so critical to everything, from our professional and personal credibility to guaranteeing the quality and reliability of our products and services. We'd get no repeat business without it and, these days, savvy audiences know how to check brands out so we might not even get a first chance.

A great way to demonstrate authenticity is to showcase supportive content, such as reviews, from your existing audience, be they employees or customers. Why?

Because the online audience considers content from individuals to be more authentic than that shared by brands themselves.

If you don't have employees, this means sharing your own thoughts as an individual and the reviews and recommendations your clients leave for you.

In fact, content shared by employees receives 8x the engagement and gets re-shared 24 times more frequently than the same content shared directly by the brand. (LinkedIn)

Write your brand story.
Start from the moment you conceived your business idea and tell your story, warts and all.

Make sure everything you post has a purpose that relates back to your brand, values, and key messages.

B is for Brand

Let's not underestimate the importance of spending time and budget on creating a strong, original and engaging brand for your business.

It's about so much more than simply a logo; you need a clear value proposition and messaging to go with it. Your tone of voice is important and will largely be driven by an understanding of your ideal target audience, or avatar.

Preparation is key in developing all these elements of your brand but, the good news is, doing so properly will give you plenty of content to be getting on with.

People love a back story and your route to finding the perfect brand is just that. Your brand is an extension of you and may share your core values.

Try using your values as topic generators for blogs or curated content. You're aiming for an instantly recognisable brand identity which brings content your audience expects to see, but which still delights and entertains them.

Keep a list of useful
sources of supportive content.

Only ever share from
reputable/quality/values-driven
websites and always give credit.

Never give extra reach to fake news.

C is for Curation

Ok, so content curation is a bit of an industry buzzword but it's an important concept to get familiar with.

In a nutshell this is all about annexing content from elsewhere to enrich your feeds.

Of course, I'm not suggesting you copy other peoples' blogs and posts but you can use them to illustrate and lend credibility to your messages. They introduce variety to your narrative, which adds more value to your audience.

Key things to remember with curation:
- Use credible sources.
- If you're trying to underline a point, better to share from a recognisable leader in the field than an unknown hobby blogger, for obvious reasons.
- Always make sure you add comments to anything you share. Your audience will switch off if they visit your page or profile and only find forwarded posts with other people's thoughts on them.
- Show why you are sharing and explain what value you think the information brings to your audience.

90% of B2B buyers say online content has influenced their purchase decision

Notes

Know your value proposition inside out. Why are you different from your competitors?

Now share it widely but don't be a pushy sales person, make your case more subtly by talking about where you can add value.

D is for Differentiate

This is marketing speak for 'stand out from the crowd'.

You need to give your followers the excuse they need to do business with you. It's not so much 'why should I buy from you?' but more 'why should I buy from you NOW?'

Convincing and converting are the trickiest parts of content writing to get right and you need to do your research and be confident in what you deliver that others can't.

Marketers would call this your USP (Unique Selling Point) and you need to include it in your messaging.

One way to do this really effectively is to turn your posting style on its head and write about your customer's pain point. What is it that's keeping them awake at night?

Start with this and you'll definitely get their attention. It's often then easier to identify how you'll solve this problem and therefore why they need your product or service in their life.

Emotion tip:
share within your comfort zone.
Remember what goes on social, stays on social.

Be proud of your journey and what you've achieved.

E is for Emotion

Heads up, here comes a cliché; "people buy people".

Well, they do say phrases become clichés for a reason and this one is proven repeatedly by the popularity of individuals over brands.

By speaking as the person behind the business, and letting your employees do the same, you're humanising your brand. Your followers can see that you have a passion and a purpose and that's the sort of thing that makes them want to do business with you.

It's often easier for smaller brands to show their personable side. They might have the local angle or an unusual provenance.

It's also a little about showing vulnerability. As soon as we do this through our content, people empathise and can see we're just like them. Vulnerability builds trust and trust wins business.

F can also be for 'frequency'.

Consistency is a winner when it comes to content creation.

Avoid feast and famine and try to create little and often.

F is for Fire-in-your-belly

So, there are some buzzwords I'm not willing to entertain, and 'Passion' is one of them. But that doesn't mean you shouldn't be conveying your energy and enthusiasm in everything you write.

It's an overused word because it matters.

Writing engaging content is about captivating your audience, keeping them reading and then convincing them to do business with you. There's no way anyone can produce sufficient content and entertainment for their audience without this fire.

When you post, you need to channel your enthusiasm, show your belief in what you do, and demonstrate your desire to make a difference. It's contagious and taking this approach will quickly help you find your audience.

It creates FOMO, it sets you up for success and it makes people want to join you on that journey.

"the idea is to write it so that people hear it and it slides through the brain and goes straight to the heart."

Maya Angelou

Notes

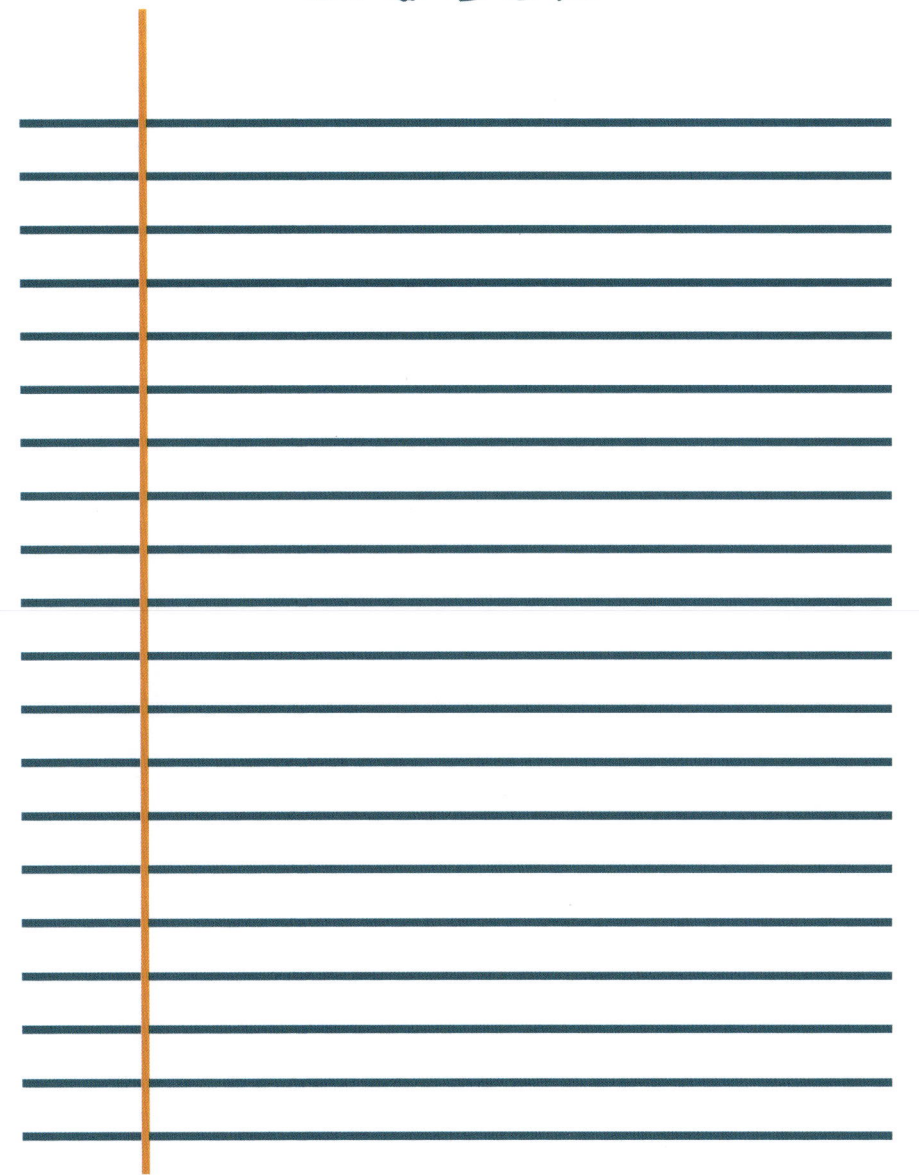

Remember less is more.
If you're time-poor, focus on fewer,
higher quality posts and really make
them echo your brand.

Engagement and outcomes will improve
as a result.

G is for Get Planning

Scatter-gunning is time consuming and yields little in the way of results when it comes to social media posting or blogging.

Consistency is the secret to success, even if you end up posting less.

Allocate some time to planning your monthly online activity and content. It'll actually save you time in the long run.

To focus your mind, try thinking of each income stream your business has, as well as each ideal client avatar you have developed. Then you have a matrix and can jot down the key messages for each sector.

What would you tell them if you had their undivided attention for a couple of minutes?

This forms the start of a framework for content writing.

Lists and questions are great ways to make your headline engaging.

Handily, they're often quicker to pull together as a blog post too.

Something like 'My top 5 tips for blogging' is a quick and easy headline so start with this style of post.

H is for Headlines

If there's ever a time when first impressions mattered, this is it.

So much has been written about which headlines make for click-ability - which encourages your audience to read them.

Headlines are, in my humble opinion, best written last unless you want to see off half a day of valuable working time, and ideally need to be informative and highly indicative of what's in the article, always including a keyword or phrase.

Think of them like a 'hook' which grabs attention and makes the reader want to know more.

Finally, keep them simple. Trying to be too clever can result in confusion and will reduce the chance of people reading on.

Use all the metrics available to you but make sure you understand their true meaning.

Engagement is still the best indicator that someone is interested in what you have to say.

I is for Insights

When you're looking at how well your content is doing, you need to ignore the likes and loves.

These are known as vanity metrics.

It's great to know people loved your picture but has it really had an impact on their opinion of the product or service you're selling? Possibly not.

Engagement and actions are the best indicator of whether a prospect is interested in doing business. If they comment, make sure you reply.

If they visit your website, keep a track of what is interesting them and you can then use this to fine-tune your future content.

"Easy reading is damn hard writing"

Nathaniel Hawthorne

Notes

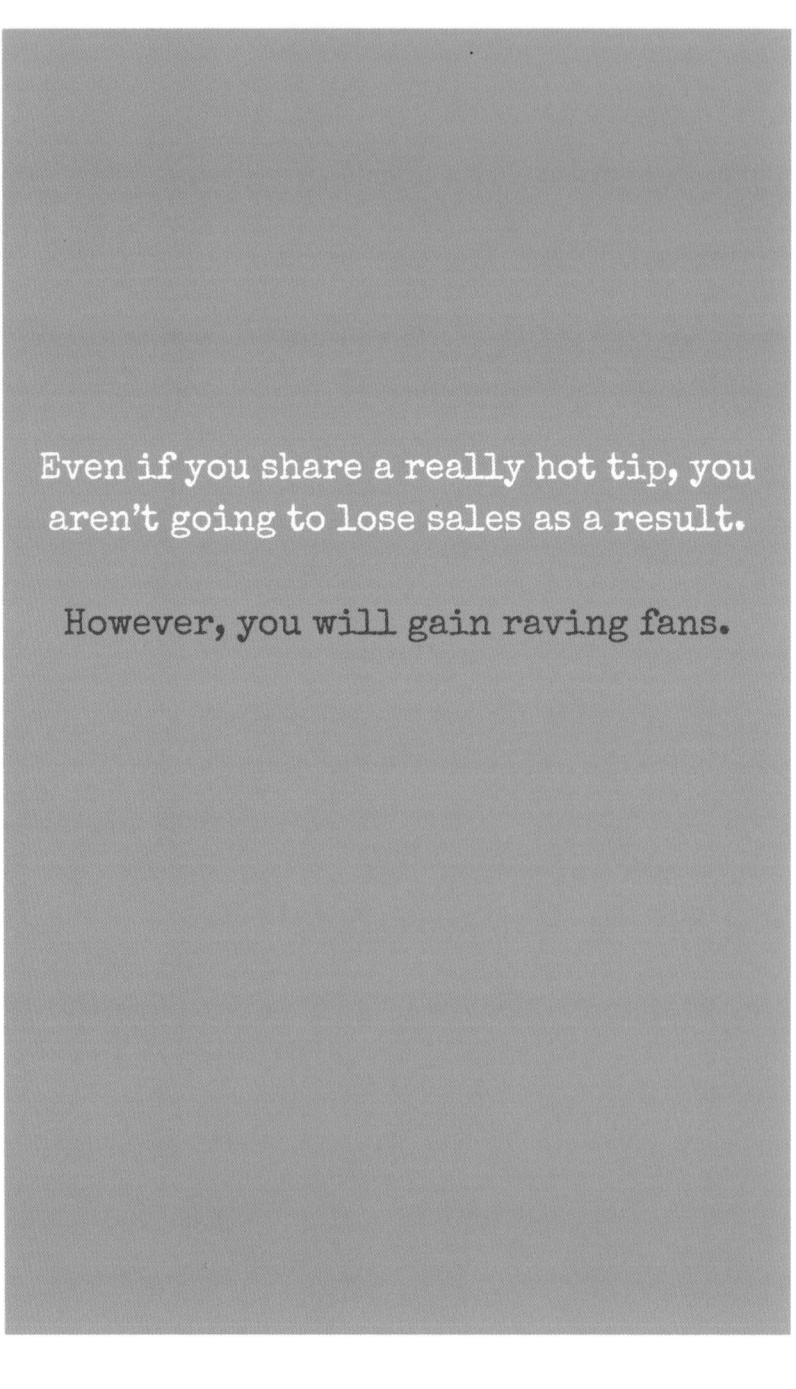

Even if you share a really hot tip, you aren't going to lose sales as a result.

However, you will gain raving fans.

J is for Just Enough

Showing you are an expert in your field is critical to gaining credibility and building an online following.

However, it can be unnerving to share your expertise and people often worry that they will 'give away their secrets'.

There's no need to worry.

One way of sharing tips but retaining some confidentiality around how you do things is to let people know what outcomes they should be aiming for but save the 'how' until they engage with you to do business.

These days, people don't pay for knowledge, they pay for the hand-holding that an expert provides to make something happen.

Building trust is the first step in building a relationship which may result in a sale.

Trust needs a few ingredients, such as vulnerability, empathy and resonance.

K is for Know Your Audience

The more time you spend working on who your ideal client is, the more likely you are to understand what they need from you.

Importantly, the more you have them (and their needs) in mind when you create content, the more your messaging will resonate with them.

So, create some avatars. Ideal clients with names, identities, personalities and challenges that you are perfectly placed to solve.

You can't spend too much time getting under the skin of your ideal client. Displaying empathy for their challenges is the start of building trust and then a relationship that could include doing business together.

Don't feel you have to stick to 'round numbers'.

Lists are often in 5s or 10s, but can be any number providing all the tips are adding value.

L is for Listicles

Listicles, often entitled 'top ten tips', 'five ways to...', and A to Z lists, are great inspiration for content.

From blog posts to downloads, people love to feel they have something they can learn from and, handily, they are quick and easy to write assuming you're focusing on your area of expertise.

It's always good to have variety but sharing a top ten type post regularly is a good way to keep your audience engaged and active.

Go back to your ideal client and list their top 5 challenges with explanations of how you can help.

Even a small amount of planning will help you post more consistently.

Use your time to work on themes which can be used throughout the year.

Themes make it easier to write future posts, saving time.

M is for Maintaining Consistency

When you are busy with client delivery, social media and other content writing often takes a back seat.

It's easy to be inconsistent, posting loads one week and nothing the next.

Unsurprisingly, this isn't the best way to engage and retain a healthy audience.

Instead, focus on quality, not quantity and put aside a small amount of time to plan.

The effort you might put into creating a flurry of posts will then serve your channels for a longer period of time.

By slowly building up a good supply of content ideas, you will remove the pressure to create every day and make the whole process more enjoyable.

"All things being equal, people will do business with, and refer business to, those people they know, like and trust."

Bob Burg

Notes

The main ways to nurture and grow relationships are to comment, share and engage with others' content as well as spending time on your own posts.

Try to spend a little time on engagement every day.

N is for Nurturing

Business communications need to be two-way.

You are creating content to attract and retain an audience of prospective customers.

Good relationship building is critical to success in today's ultra-competitive world, where more and more business is done online.

The more time you spend on building and nurturing your relationships, the better conversion rates you will achieve.

In the context of content, nurturing means thinking about different ways to engage your audience. You might choose a variety of channels and content styles.

For example. as well as posting on social media, your content can be used in direct email marketing, content campaigns, on newsletters, and can be produced as written content, or in videos or podcasts.

Using a selection and repurposing your messages is a powerful way to market your business.

Offers are a great way to add people to your marketing lists by asking them to sign up to receive something.

You will then know what sort of information they are interested in and can tailor future content accordingly.

O is for Offers

Offers are about giving your audience an incentive to engage with you, and don't always mean reducing your prices.

I prefer to focus on adding further value. Can you repurpose something into a download or cheat sheet?

Think about sharing tips, advice, free merchandise, downloads or reports.

These will add real value and provide a platform for you to build on for business growth.

Offers help to deal with convincing your audience to make a buying decision now, not put it off until later.

Steer clear of those taboo topics like politics unless they're integral to your business.

You're aiming for conversion, not controversy.

P is for Positivity

Your content should always be authentic and balanced, but it is good practice to stay positive when it comes to the topics you cover.

I'm talking about the usual culprits such as politics and religion. Unless they are directly related to your business, it can be risky to include them in your content (not to mention irrelevant).

Don't forget, you want to create visibility for your brand, not chase attention. Being controversial is not the way to do that so sharing anything that could divide opinion might be a risk.

Try to balance good and bad news and don't engage in debates with any keyboard warriors.

The same goes for publishing rants when something gets your goat. It's a risky strategy although it can work if you are championing a strongly held opinion in your line of work.

Think it through carefully, ask yourself whether it truly adds value and, if in doubt, don't.

Questions, polls and votes are excellent for engagement and can provide useful market research.

Use them to ask a pertinent question and then write a blog post sharing and explaining the answers.

Q is for Questions

Questions – whether you ask them or answer them, are a great addition to your content mix.

They enable you to address almost anything and are great for engagement and to showcase your knowledge.

They convey that you are genuinely interested in your audience – but don't forget to engage with responses if you pose a question in your post.

Use your ideal client research to help decide on a question that you know is an issue.

Find out what people think, provide some pearls of wisdom and even run an 'ask me anything' slot where people can submit questions related to your sphere of expertise.

It's easy to think our social media posts are seen by all our audience.

That's not the case, so don't be afraid to repurpose using rephrasing or different images.

Repetition is key to good reach.

R is for Repurposing

Anyone who's ever studied marketing will be familiar with the concept that people need to see something multiple times before they take action.

Our content is seen by a small proportion of our audience and it is thought that only 3% of them are ready to buy at that moment.

That's a frighteningly small number but it illustrates why we need to be visible and continue to convince and convert.

Repurposing is about reusing your inspirational content ideas in more than one post or place.

Repeat your message and hammer it home. It's not nagging, it's reminding people that you have an amazing product or service which can really help them.

"Brands will need to develop their own personality and set of values in order to be able to have meaningful one-on-one interactions. That's how they will stand out in a world of noise and limited attention."
HubSpot

Notes

Whenever you consider posting a piece of content, consider who it will help and how.

Everything you do online should build towards expertise, education around your product or service and raising the profile of your brand.

S is for Social Selling

Did you know that today's buyer admits to viewing, on average, five different pieces of content before selecting their supplier?

The buying journey has changed: people no longer want to hear you sell. They want to know what value you can add.

They want to be educated, they want proof of how your product or service can help them overcome their challenge.

Building and nurturing relationships is social selling.

By creating a variety of content which educates and entertains, you are positioning your brand in the front of the minds of people following you.

And you're setting yourself up as an expert in your field.

If you publish a blog containing tips, break them down and share one a day on another channel, such as Instagram or Facebook.

This repurposes your content and drives more traffic to your original blog post.

T is for Top Tips

Sharing tips is about showing you understand and empathise with your prospective customers.

It's a great way to show you know what you are talking about, without necessarily giving away your secret recipe.

It enables people to 'try before they buy' when it comes to your advice and approach.

It generates interest and new followers and works well with the listicle style post that we mentioned earlier.

*Semrush

34% of buyers will make an unplanned purchase after reading quality content*

Notes

Stick to short sentences and simple language to get your point across.

Use testimonials and case studies to illustrate the points you make.

This helps make things real for your audience.

U is for Understanding

Understanding is relevant in two ways.

Firstly, you can demonstrate you understand the challenges being faced by prospective customers and create your content accordingly, showing how you can solve their problem.

Secondly, and perhaps more importantly, you need people to understand what you are telling them.

Stick to simple, jargon-free language when writing content and tell them just what they need to know, nothing more.

Too much technical detail will confuse them and a confused mind says 'no'.

Bring your energy to
a video by recording yourself straight
after an event or experience.

You might have sold your first product
or package, taken on a new client, or
attended a fantastic conference.

Get straight on camera and enthuse;
your audience will love the energy.

V is for Videoing

A hugely popular format, video is a great addition to your content mix.

However, if the thought if it makes you want to run for the hills, start small. The good news is the days of overly professional and polished video are gone.

Try out the tip I share opposite for your first attempt.

'Explainer videos' are an option if you want to stay out of shot, though, take people through how a product or service works by recording your screen on Zoom or showing a demonstration taking place.

Weave your 'why' in among other content to keep the personal element to your business.

People buy people and your story will help you gain trust and show authenticity.

W is for Why

If you own your own business, your 'why' is likely to be one of the most powerful stories you can tell.

People usually branch out alone either because they've got a passion to make a difference or because they want a lifestyle change.

Telling your audience about your 'why' will humanise your brand.

It will help people to identify with you and give them a reason to buy from you and not a competitor.

When you're brainstorming your 'why' think about the emotional outcomes of what you do as well as the business ones. It's good to have a balance of elements in your content to appeal to different people.

Try using FAQs if you have a particularly complex message to get across.

They are often easier to write clearly as you can pose the exact question you want to answer.

X is for eXplain

There's a balance to be struck when it comes to explaining what you do.

Too much detail, especially if it's 'technical' will lose your audience but too little could make you sound inexperienced.

You only need to include details that differentiate your product and form part of the decision-making process for buyers. They don't always need to know every detail of how you achieve what you do.

However, it is important to include the information that people need to know about working with you.

Qualifying criteria or prerequisites for signing up shouldn't be omitted.

A good way to show a little of yourself but stay professional is to be interviewed.

The interview could be in video format or you could turn it into a blog post.

Y is for You

As a business owner, you are your brand.

It's so important to show the human side of your brand so, from time to time, share something from behind the scenes.

As humans, we're inherently nosey, and we love a peek behind the curtain so this could involve showing people how you prepare, plan or even relax outside of work.

Choose what feels comfortable, social media can be a window into your life but only as much as you want it to.

If you're struggling to focus on writing content, use the Pomodoro Technique.

Set a timer for 25 minutes and work on one thing only during that time.

When the buzzer goes, either reset it for more time or move on to another task.

Z is for The Zone

We all work differently and it's important to understand what days and times are good for creativity when it comes to producing content.

Are you a morning person or a night owl?

Plan your week around the times you feel most creative.

There's no point in forcing things – you'll end up frustrated and still with a blank sheet of paper.

Once you know what works best for you, block the time out on a regular basis and you'll soon find you love your content creation sessions.

*LinkedIn

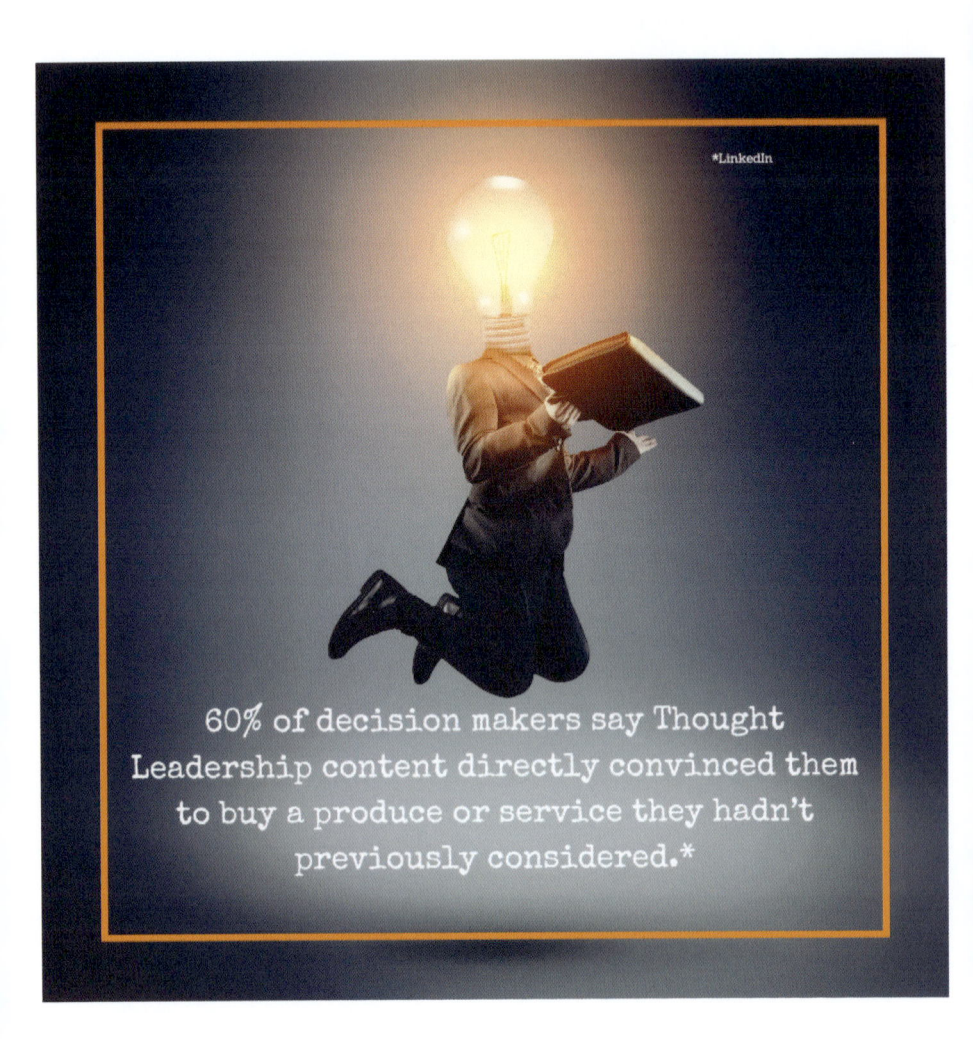

60% of decision makers say Thought Leadership content directly convinced them to buy a produce or service they hadn't previously considered.*

Notes

Notes

Notes

About the author

Emma Rundle is founder and owner of Melting Pot Creations, a copy and content writing agency which writes creative and engaging copy for small and medium-sized businesses who want to grow by establishing a strong and authentic online presence.

She lives in Northamptonshire with her two daughters.

www.meltingpotcreations.co.uk

Printed in Great Britain
by Amazon